My First Book about Elephants

I0439613

Amazing Animal Books
Children's Picture Books

By Molly Davidson

Mendon Cottage Books

JD-Biz Publishing

Download Free Books!
http://MendonCottageBooks.com

Read More Amazing Animal Books

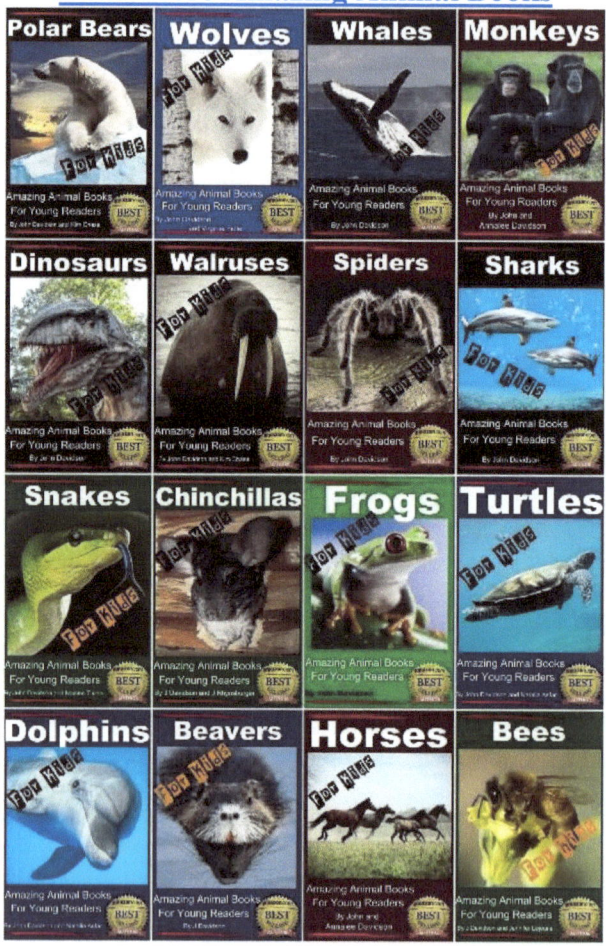

Purchase at Amazon.com
Download Free Books!
http://MendonCottageBooks.com

Table of Contents

Introduction 4
About Elephants 6
The Evolution of Elephants 8
Elephant Features 10
Where Elephants Live 13
How Elephants Eat...15
How Elephants Talk...17
Life In The Herd...20
African Elephants..22
Asian Elephants..23
Fun Elephant Facts...25
Publisher...34

Introduction

Elephants have a very good memory, some scientists believe it is even better than a human's memory.

Elephants are realtives of the exctinct ice age Mammoth.

Elephants are NOT afraid of mice, like you may have heard.

An elephant's tusks can be different lengths.

Girls will stay in a herd their whole life, but a boy will usually live by itself after it turns 14 years old.

About Elephants

There was a long time ago over 350 different species of elephant, now there is only two, the African and Asian elephants.

The Asian elephants have smaller bodies and bigger ears than the African elephants.

Both the boy and the girl African elephant grow tusks, but only the boy Asian elephants do.

Scientists have done studies on an elephants intelligence. They had them play games and watched how they played with others.

Through research they proved elepants have the greatest memory of anything on earth.

The Evolution of Elephants

After much research, it is proven that elephants are relatives to the extinct Mammoth.

One big difference is Mammoths have a thick coat which helped keep them warm, elephants do not need to keep warm.

Elephanst actually have much larger ears than the Mammoth did, this helps keep them cool.

The first history of elephants is in about 2000 B.C.

Elephants were used to help build buildings, because they are so big and strong.

Elephant Features

An elephant's trunk is its most important feature; it has over 40,000 muscles in it.

They use them to smell, to pick up objects, to talk, and they can even uproot a large tree with it.

Elephants have 24 teeth and 2 tusks.

Their tusks never stop growing, this is how you can tell how old an elephant is, by looking at how long thier tusks are.

They use their tusks to dig for water, or to scrap bark from a tree, so they can eat the tree pulp.

Elephants cannot run, they will just walk slowly for hours and hours, to get where they need to go.

An elephant's skin is about one inch thick.

To help keep itself cool, it will flap its large ears, which act like a fan.

Where Elephants Live

Elephants live in many different places like the Savannah Desert, grasslands, forests, and swamps.

Wild elephants today only live in Africa and Asia, in tropical regions.

Elephants have bad eyesight, so it makes it hard to find food in the nighttime.

They like to live where there is a least 12 hours of daylight per day, this gives them enough time to find food, in the light.

Elephants migrate every year from one place to another, in search of food.

They travel between 12 - 21 miles per day.

How Elephants Eat

Elephants can eat up to 50 tons of plants every year, including leaves, twigs, roots, grass, and fruit.

They use their trunks to grab food that is high in the trees.

If they cannnot rech what they want they will shake the tree until the fruit falls down.

If this doesn't work, they will rip the tree out of the ground, then eat it.

At one time, an elepant can drink almost 4 gallons of water through their trunks!

During the dry season it is hard for them to find enough water, so they will use their trunks to dig down and find water.

How Elephants Talk

One way elephants talk to each other is by a loud trumpeting sound; it can be heard from many miles away.

Young elephants, called calves, learn their mothers trumpeting noise so they can easily find them.

They also make low growling or grunting noises.

Another way elephants talk is without sound, it's by touch. They may wrap their trunks around each other to show excitement or love.

Elephants also rub their bodies together, this is like a hug or hand shake.

If an elephant has their trunk in the air, this can be a warning that they may fight.

Life In The Herd

Girl elephants will stay with the same herd their whole life, and they are friendly to all elephants, even those not in her herd.

Boy elephants walk on the outside of the herd when traveling to help protect the girls and babies on the inside.

As boys get older they start to leave the groups for a few days at a time, then they finally stop being with the herd and leave to live by themselves.

When there is enough food and water, the elephants will play in the herd.

Elephants are very smart, and each elephant knows its place in the herd.

African Elephants

African elephants are bigger than Asian elephants, they can be over 12 feet tall and weigh more than 14,000 pounds!

Most of them live in the Savannah Desert, in a herd of 12 - 20 elephants.

Asian Elephants

In the Asian culture, elephants are looked up to as a sign of wisdom, intelligence, and strength.

Asian elephants have smaller ears than the African elephant.

They are about 12 feet tall, and weigh about 11,000 pounds.

Young Asian elephants enjoying a swim

Asian elephants live in India, Sri Lanka, Bangladesh, Nepal, Indonesia, and Indochina.

Fun Elephant Facts

An elephants tusks can be a long as 10 feet and weigh almost 200 pounds.

Elephants have the biggest brain when compared to other land animals, it weighs 11 pounds.

A newborn calf can weigh up to 260 pounds, and is born blind.

Elephants can hear and smell really well, but they cannot see very good.

Elephants can live 50 - 70 years in the wild.

The word elephant means ivory, for their ivory tusks.

Elephants eat between 300 - 600 pounds of food per day, and drink up to 50 gallons of water.

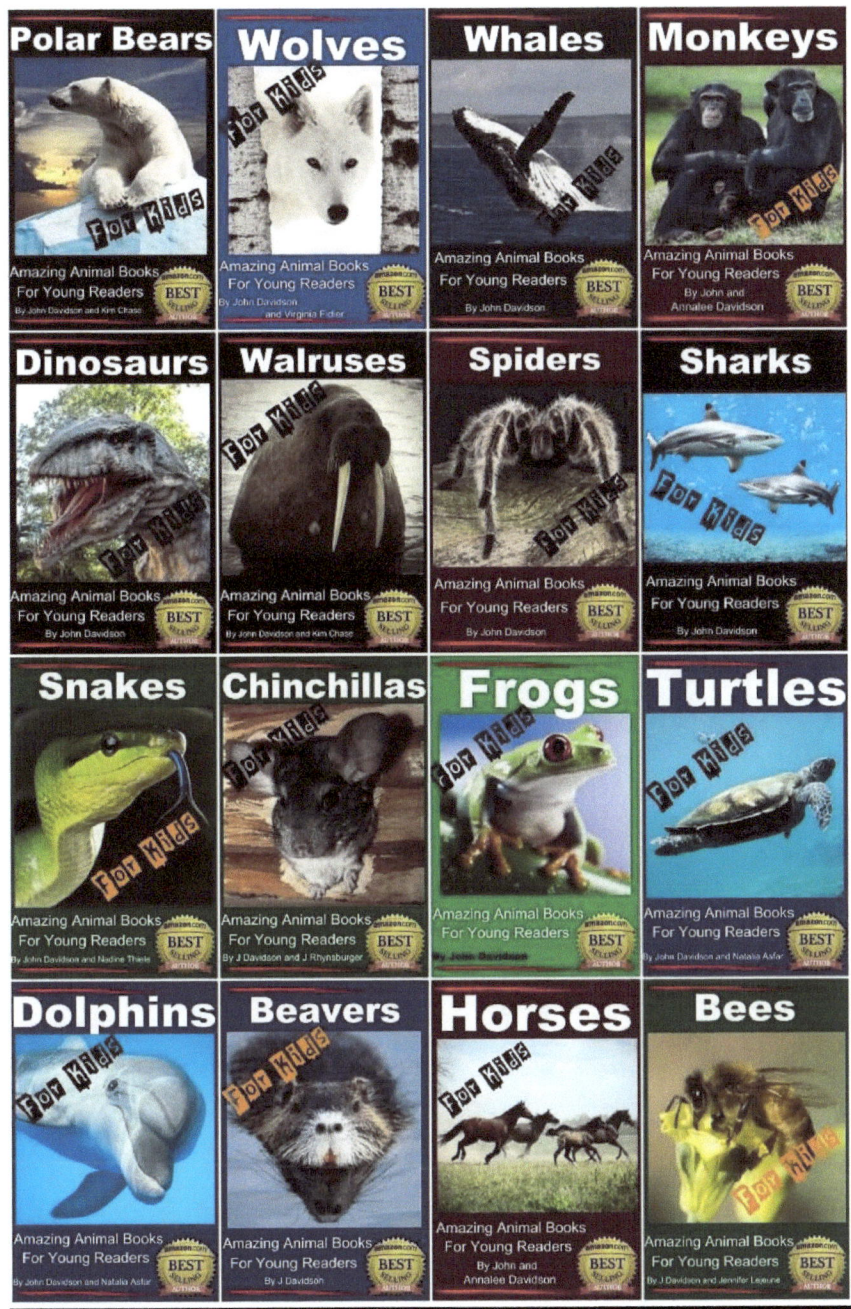

Our books are available at

1. Amazon.com
2. Barnes and Noble
3. Itunes
4. Kobo
5. Smashwords
6. Google Play Books

Download Free Books!
http://MendonCottageBooks.com

Publisher

JD-Biz Corp

P O Box 374

Mendon, Utah 84325

http://www.jd-biz.com/

Mendon Cottage Books

P O Box 374, Mendon Utah 84325

www.ingramcontent.com/pod-product-compliance
Lightning Source LLC
Chambersburg PA
CBHW050908290526
45792CB00002B/735